Phonics Vowels

Vowel Sounds
you need to know
to be a successful reader

Written by Shannon Keeley • Illustrated by Dave Garbot

Flash Kids

ISBN-13: 978-1-4114-9877-8
ISBN-10: 1-4114-9877-1

For more information please visit *www.flashkidsbooks.com*
Please submit changes or report errors to *www.flashkidsbooks.com/errors*

Printed and bound in China

Spark Publishing
120 Fifth Avenue
New York, NY 10011

Dear Parent,

Knowing vowel letters and their sounds is an important step in learning to read. This book provides fun activities that introduce vowel sounds and their letter combinations. The activities will help your child identify both short vowels and long vowels. Through tracing and writing, matching, games, mazes, and stories, your child will receive lots of practice distinguishing between the different vowel sounds. These activities build reading skills and give your child opportunities to decode words, phrases, and sentences. To get the most from the activities, follow these simple steps:

- Find a comfortable place where you and your child can work quietly together.

- Encourage your child to go at his or her own pace.

- Help your child with if he or she gets stuck.

- Offer lots of praise and support.

- Most of all, remember that learning should be fun! Take time to enjoy this special time spent together.

Visit us at *www.flashkidsbooks.com* for free downloads, informative articles, and valuable parent resources!

a You hear the short a sound in the middle of cap.

cap

Say the name of each picture and listen to the short a sound. Trace the letter a to complete the word.

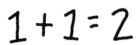

add

ant

can

dad

fast

pan

tap

wag

Tic-Tac-Toad

Say the name of each picture. Write a if it makes the short a sound. Circle the row with three short a sounds.

Circle the set of words for the three pictures in the winning row.

apple
fast
add

wag
add
fast

add
tap
cap

Ready, Set, Rhyme!

Find the name for each picture in the word list below. Write it on the line. Then draw a line to connect the pictures whose names rhyme.

cap   tap

dad   add

pan   can

Read and Number

Read each sentence and find the matching picture.
Write the number by the sentence.

_____ The ant is on the apple.

_____ Dad has a pan.

_____ The ant is on the can.

_____ Dad is fast.

You hear the short e sound in the middle of bed.

bed

Say the name of each picture and listen to the short e sound. Trace the letter e to complete the word.

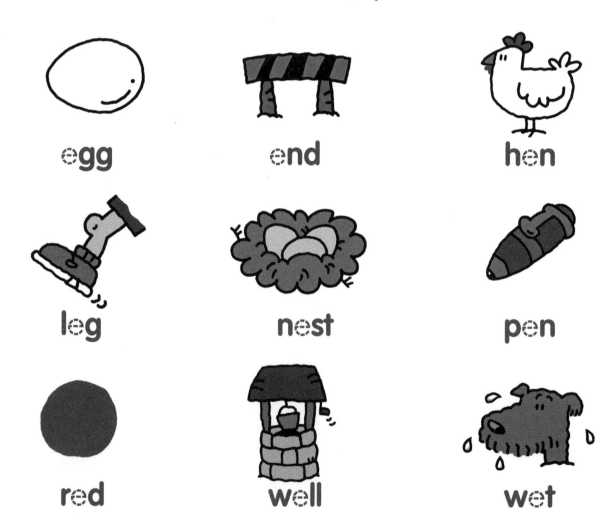

egg

end

hen

leg

nest

pen

red

well

wet

Mail Trail

Where will the mailman deliver his letter? Find the trail of pictures whose names make the short e sound. All the boxes on the trail must be touching. Write the letter e in each box along the trail.

Look at the pictures along the mailman's trail. Circle the words that name those pictures.

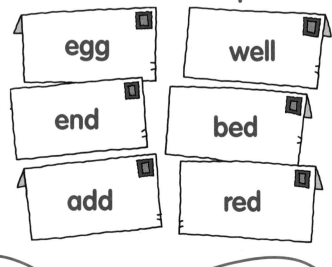

egg   well

end   bed

add   red

Ready, Set, Rhyme!

Find the name for each picture in the word list below. Write it on the line. Then draw a line to connect the pictures whose names rhyme.

pen   egg

red   leg

hen   bed

Draw a Line

Read each sentence and draw a line to the matching picture.

The hen has an egg.

The hen is wet.

The egg is in the nest.

The pen is in the nest.

Same or Different?

Say the name of each picture and write a or e. Circle the word "same" if both pictures in the pair make the same sound. Circle "different" if they make different sounds.

Race Time

Write a or e to complete each word. Count the number of short a words and the number of short e words on the race track. Write the numbers in the boxes and see which letter wins!

Start

Finish

Scoreboard

a

e

1. r__d
2. d__d
3. c__n
4. h__n
5. __gg
6. __pple
7. __nt
8. c__p

You hear the short i sound in the middle of pig.

pig

Say the name of each picture and listen to the short i sound. Trace the letter i to complete the word.

hit

inch

sick

ship

sit

sip

swim

wig

zip

Tic-Tac-Toad

Say the name of each picture. Write i if it makes the short i sound. Circle the row with three short i sounds.

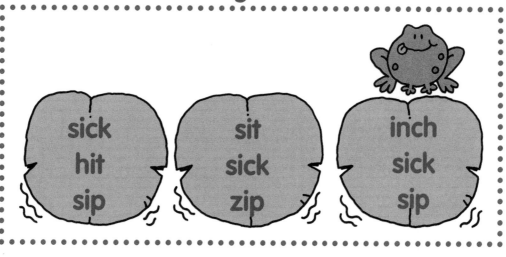

Circle the set of words for the three pictures in the winning row.

sick
hit
sip

sit
sick
zip

inch
sick
sip

Ready, Set, Rhyme!

Find the name for each picture in the word list below. Write it on the line. Then draw a line to connect the pictures whose names rhyme.

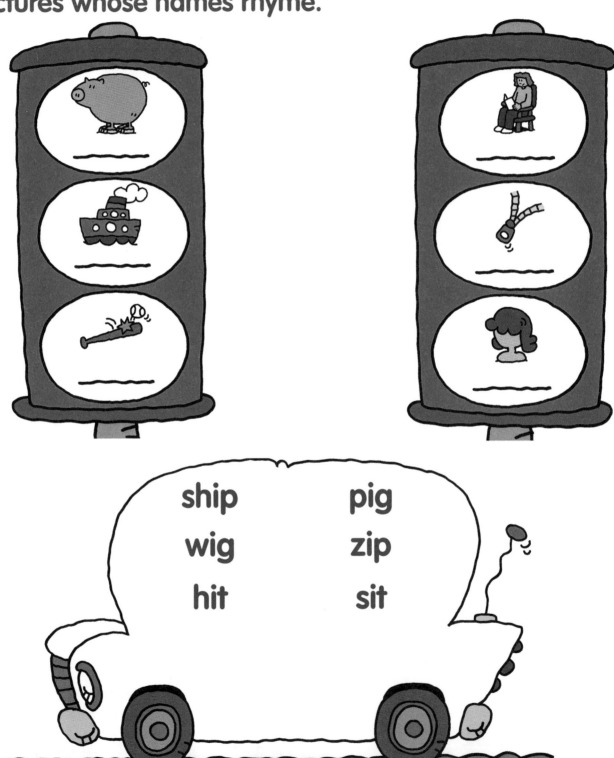

ship   pig

wig   zip

hit   sit

Read and Number

Read each sentence and find the matching picture.
Write the number by the sentence.

_____ The pig has a wig.

_____ I swim to the ship.

_____ The pig is on the ship.

_____ I swim in a wig.

Sounds and Signs

Say the name of each picture. Draw a line to connect the picture with short e or short i.

Hats Off!

Write e or i to complete each word. Then match each hat with its owner. If the word has the short e sound, draw a line to Ted. If it has the short i sound, draw a line to Tim.

sh__p

__nch

__nd

p__n

Ted

Tim

z__p

l__g

h__t

s__t

You hear the short o sound in the middle of log.

log

Say the name of each picture and listen to the short o sound. Trace the letter o to complete the word.

cl o ck

c o b

fr o g

l o ck

j o g

m o m

p o p

p o nd

st o p

Mail Trail

Where will the mailman deliver his letter? Find the trail of pictures whose names make the short o sound. All the boxes on the trail must be touching. Write the letter o in each box along the trail.

Look at the pictures along the mailman's trail. Circle the words that name those pictures.

jog

cob

stop

lock

pop

pond

Ready, Set, Rhyme!

Draw a line to connect the pictures whose names rhyme. Write it on the line. Find the name for each picture in the word list below.

frog   clock

pop   jog

stop   lock

Draw a Line

Read each sentence and draw a line to the matching picture.

 **The frog is on the log.**

 **The frog is on the lock.**

 **Mom has a clock.**

 **Mom has a cob.**

Same or Different?

Say the name of each picture and write i or o. Circle the word "same" if both pictures in the pair make the same sound. Circle "different" if they make different sounds.

1. STOP   same different

2. same different

3. same different

4. same different

5. same different

6. same different

Race Time

Write i or o to complete each word. Count the number of short i words and the number of short o words on the race track. Write the numbers in the boxes and see which letter wins!

Start

Finish

1. sh__p

2. s__t

3. l__ck

4. z__p

5. l__g

6. __nch

7. p__nd

8. sw__m

Scoreboard

i

o

U

You hear the short u sound in the middle of sun.

sun

Say the name of each picture and listen to the short u sound. Trace the letter u to complete the word.

duck

fun

jump

mug

plug

pup

sub

truck

up

Tic-Tac-Toad

Say the name of each picture. Write u if it makes the short u sound. Circle the row with three short u sounds.

Circle the set of words for the three pictures in the winning row.

jump
plug
sub

up
duck
plug

jump
up
inch

Ready, Set, Rhyme!

Find the name for each picture in the word list below. Write it on the line. Then draw a line to connect the pictures whose names rhyme.

fun   up

pup   mug

sun   plug

Read and Number

Read each sentence and find the matching picture.
Write the number by the sentence.

_____ The duck is in the truck.

_____ The mug is in the sun.

_____ The pup is in the truck.

_____ The sub is in the sun.

Sounds and Signs

Say the name of each picture. Draw a line to connect the picture with short o or short u.

Hats Off!

Write o or u to complete each word. Then match each hat with its owner. If the word has the short o sound, draw a line to Bob. If it has the short u sound, draw a line to Gus.

STOP

tr__ck

st__p

s__b

__p

Bob

Gus

c__b

s__n

p__nd

l__ck

Same or Different?

Say the name of each picture and write u or a. Circle the word "same" if both pictures in the pair make the same sound. Circle "different" if they make different sounds.

1. same different

2. same different

3. same different

4. same different

5. same different

6. same different

Race Time

Write u or a to complete each word. Count the number of short u words and the number of short a words on the race track. Write the numbers in the boxes and see which letter wins!

Start

Finish

1. __nt

2. j__mp

3. m__g

4. __pple

5. c__p

6. pl__g

7. s__b

8. s__n

Scoreboard

u

a

Rainy Review

Draw a line to connect the pictures whose names make the same vowel sound.

What Belongs in the Box?

Say the name of the pictures in each box. Cross out the picture whose name does not make the same sound as the other two. Then write the correct sound in the box.

Gumball Fun

Write the missing vowel for each word.

1. pl__g

2. f__n

3. h__t

4. r__d

5. d__d

6. z__p

7. p__n

8. w__g

9. __nd

10. s__b

11. fr__g

Picture Search

Search the scene and find two pictures for each short vowel sound. Circle the pictures and write the words below.

can	apple	wet	leg	sip
zip	clock	cob	pup	sun

a   e   i   o   u

___ ___ ___ ___ ___

Which Word?

Circle the word that matches the picture. Then write the word on the line.

1. _____
   wag wig

2. _____
   pop pup

3. _____
   leg log

4. _____
   fast nest

5. _____
   end add

6. _____
   cob cap

Crossword Puzzle

Use the picture clues to complete the puzzle.

Down

1.
4.
5.
7.
8.

Across

2.
3.
6.
8.
9.

Story Time

Write the word to complete each sentence in the story.

| fast | cap | frog | jump | pond | wet |

1. The pup has my _____.

2. He is too _____.

3. He sees a _____ jump.

4. Stop, pup. Don't _____!

5. The pup is in the _____.

6. Now my cap is all _____.

Picture This

Draw a line to match each sentence with the correct picture.

Dad can jog.
Dad can swim.

Mom has a pen.
Mom has a pan.

The ant is on the log.
The ant is on the mug.

Draw a picture to match each sentence. Connect the sentence and the picture.

The pig has an apple.
The pig has a cob.

a_e

Cake makes the long a sound.

cake

Say the name of each picture and listen to the long a sound. Circle the letters a and e in each word.

bake

cane

cape

cave

lake

race

Now trace the letters a and e in each word.

rake

skate

tape

Monkey Maze

Help the monkey find its way through the maze. Connect the pictures whose names make the long a sound.

Which pictures did you connect in the maze? Circle the words that name those pictures.

bake

cape

race

lake

rake

All Aboard

Say the name of each picture in the train. Find the word that matches each picture and write it on the line.

skate
cane
cave

_____

_____

_____

_____

_____

_____

bake
rake
race

cake
tape
cape

_____

_____

_____

Silly Sentences

Circle the sentence that matches each picture.

1.
a) The cake is in the cave.
b) The rake is in the cave.

2.
a) We race around the rake.
b) We race around the lake.

3.
a) I skate in a cape.
b) I skate in a cave.

4.
a) Tape is on the cane.
b) Tape is on the cake.

ai Rain makes the long a sound.

rain

Say the name of each picture and listen to the long a sound. Circle the letters ai in each word.

bait

braid

maid

pail

paint

sail

Now trace the letters ai in each word.

snail

tail

train

Hidden Picture

Say the name of each picture. If it makes the long a sound, color the space.

Look at the pictures in the spaces you colored. Circle the words that name those pictures.

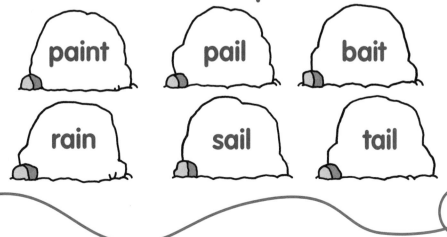

paint   pail   bait

rain   sail   tail

All Aboard

Say the name of each picture in the train. Find the word that matches each picture and write it on the line.

braid
paint
bait

tail
maid
train

pail
sail
snail

Riddles and Rhymes

Read each riddle and look at the picture. Write the word to complete the riddle.

rain   braid   pail

1. The maid has a _____.

2. The snail is on the _____.

3. The train is in the _____.

ay

Hay makes the long a sound.

hay

Say the name of each picture and listen to the long a sound. Circle the letters ay in each word.

clay

jay

May

pay

pray

ray

Now trace the letters ay in each word.

say

spray

tray

Count Down

Circle the pictures whose names make the long a sound. Count the circled pictures on each rocket and write the number. Which rocket has the higher number?

Look at the circled pictures on the winning rocket. Circle the matching words.

May   pay   spray   say   ray

All Aboard

Say the name of each picture in the train. Find the word that matches each picture and write it on the line.

pay
pray
tray

say
spray
ray

May
hay
jay

Puzzle Time

Draw a line to match each picture with the correct sentence.

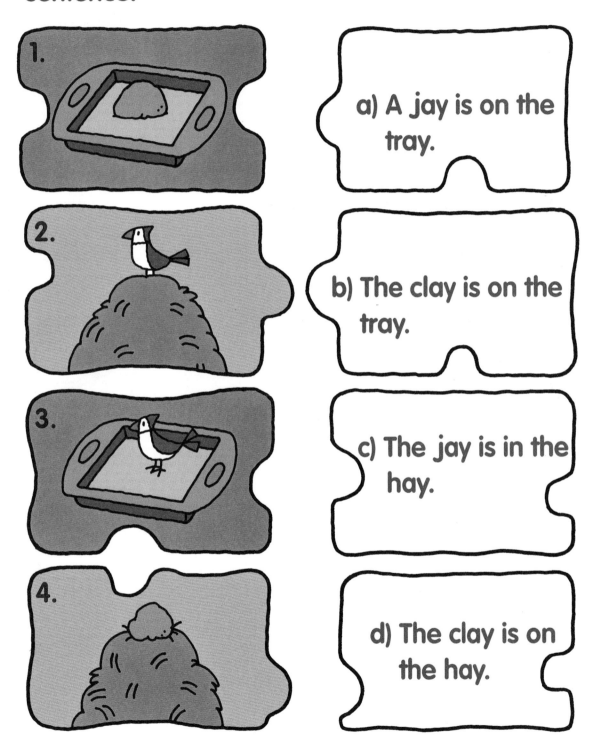

1.

a) A jay is on the tray.

2.

b) The clay is on the tray.

3.

c) The jay is in the hay.

4.

d) The clay is on the hay.

Zoo Review

Write the vowels to complete each word.

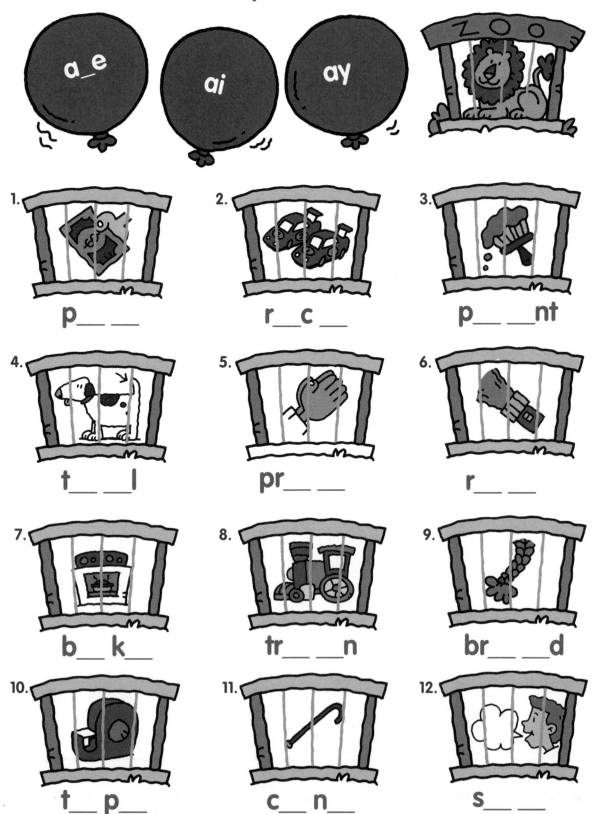

a_e   ai   ay

1. p___ ___

2. r___ c___

3. p___ ___nt

4. t___ ___l

5. pr___ ___

6. r___ ___

7. b___ k___

8. tr___ ___n

9. br___ ___d

10. t___ p___

11. c___ n___

12. s___ ___ ___

Find the Five

Find the five words that are shown in the picture and circle them. Cross out the words that are not shown in the picture.

cave	lake	hay	bait	snail
pail	sail	jay	cape	cake

ee **Bee makes the long e sound.**

bee

Say the name of each picture and listen to the long e sound. Circle the letters ee in each word.

cheek

heel

peel

sleep

sheep

three

Now trace the letters ee in each word.

tree

weed

wheel

Monkey Maze

Help the monkey find its way through the maze. Connect the pictures whose names make the long e sound.

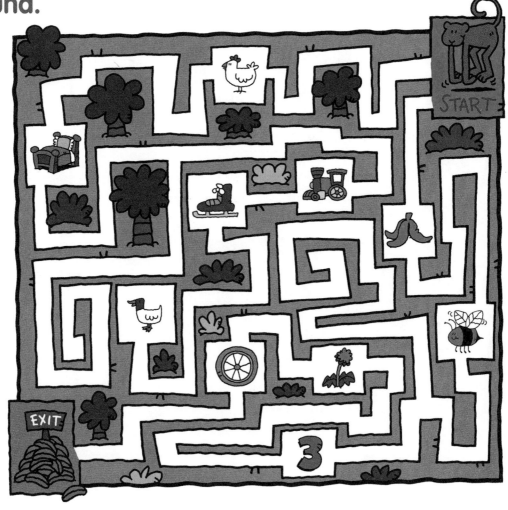

Which pictures did you connect in the maze? Circle the words that name those pictures.

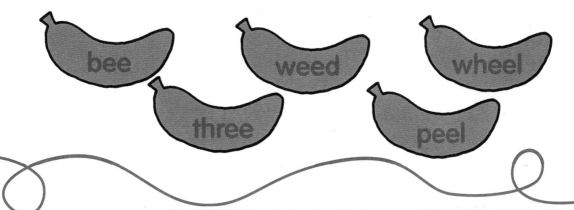

bee   weed   wheel

three   peel

All Aboard

Say the name of each picture in the train. Find the word that matches each picture and write it on the line.

cheek
sleep
sheep

wheel
heel
weed

tree
bee
three

Silly Sentences

Circle the sentence that matches each picture.

1.
a) The bee is on my heel.
b) The bee is on my cheek.

2.
a) The sheep likes to sleep.
b) The cheek likes to sleep.

3.
a) A heel is on the tree.
b) A three is on the tree.

4.
a) The peel is by the weed.
b) The peel is by the wheel.

 **ea** **Tea makes the long e sound.**

tea

Say the name of each picture and listen to the long e sound. Circle the letters ea in each word.

beach

bead

eat

ear

meat

pea

Now trace the letters ea in each word.

peach

sea

seal

Hidden Picture

Say the name of each picture. If it makes the long e sound, color the space.

Look at the pictures in the spaces you colored. Circle the words that name those pictures.

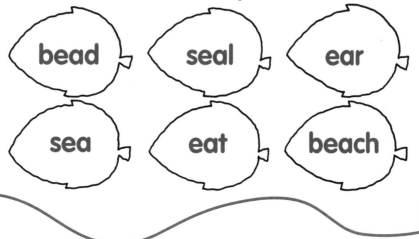

bead   seal   ear

sea   eat   beach

All Aboard

Say the name of each picture in the train. Find the word that matches each picture and write it on the line.

beach
bead
peach

seal
pea
sea

meat
eat
ear

Riddles and Rhymes

Read each riddle and look at the picture. Write the word to complete the riddle.

tea	beach	meat

1. The peach is on the _____.

2. I like to eat the _____.

3. A pea is in the _____.

Zoo Review

Write the vowels to complete each word.

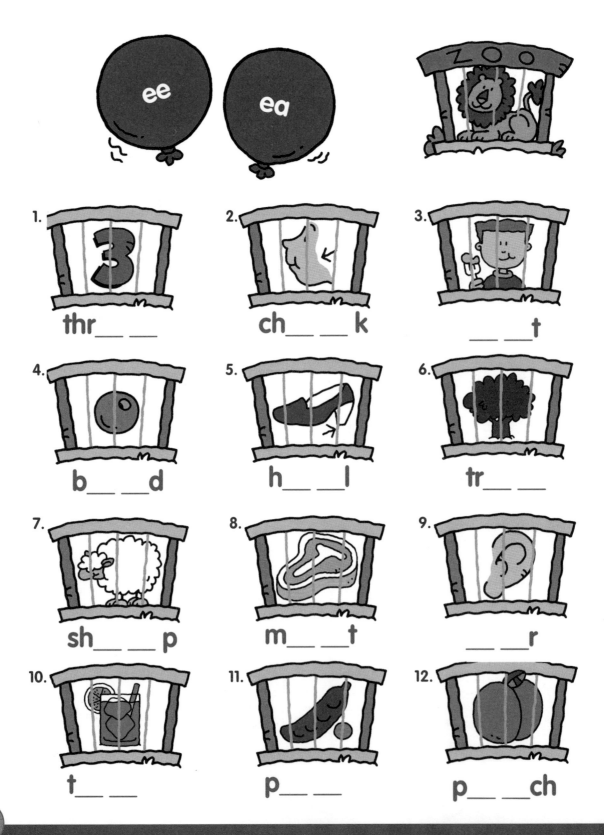

1. thr__ __

2. ch__ __ k

3. __ __t

4. b__ __d

5. h__ __l

6. tr__ __

7. sh__ __p

8. m__ __t

9. __ __r

10. t__ __

11. p__ __

12. p__ __ch

Find the Five

Find the five words that are shown in the picture and circle them. Cross out the words that are not shown in the picture.

sleep	seal	peel	wheel	bee
sea	tree	weed	beach	bead

Sounds and Signs

Say the name of each picture. Draw a line to connect the picture with long a or long e.

Hats Off!

Write the vowels to complete each word. Then match each hat with its owner. If the word has the long a sound, draw a line to Jane. If it has the long e sound, draw a line to Dee.

a_e   ai
ay   ee
ea

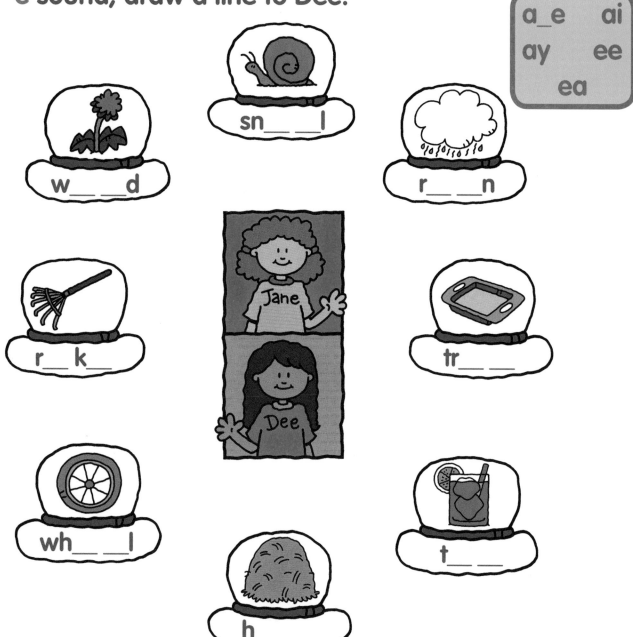

sn__ __l

w__ __ __d

r__ __n

r__k__

Jane

Dee

tr__ __ __

wh__ __l

h__ __ __

t__ __ __

 **Bike makes the long i sound.**

bike

Say the name of each picture and listen to the long i sound. Circle the letters i and e in each word.

dime

dive

hide

mice

pine

pipe

Now trace the letters i and e in each word.

pie

tie

time

Count Down

Circle the pictures whose names make the long i sound. Count the circled pictures on each rocket and write the number. Which rocket has the higher number?

Look at the circled pictures on the winning rocket. Circle the matching words.

tie

dive

hide

dime

time

All Aboard

Say the name of each picture in the train. Find the word that matches each picture and write it on the line.

pie
pine
pipe

mice
time
tie

dime
hide
dive

Puzzle Time

Draw a line to match each picture with the correct sentence.

1.

2.

3.

4.

a) The mice are on the pie.

b) The tie is on the pipe.

c) The mice are on the pine.

d) The tie is on the bike.

 **Fly makes the long i sound.**

fly

Say the name of each picture and listen to the long i sound. Circle the letter y in each word.

cry

dry

fly

fry

pry

shy

Now trace the letter y in each word.

sky

spy

why

Monkey Maze

Help the monkey find its way through the maze. Connect the pictures whose names make the long i sound.

Which pictures did you connect in the maze? Circle the words that name those pictures.

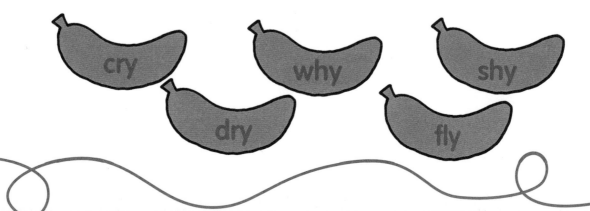

cry

why

shy

dry

fly

All Aboard

Say the name of each picture in the train. Find the word that matches each picture and write it on the line.

dry
pry
cry

_____ _____ _____

_____ _____ _____ fly
                            fry
                            why

shy
sky
spy

_____ _____ _____

Silly Sentences

Circle the sentence that matches each picture.

1.

a) The fly is in the sky.

b) The fly is shy.

2.

a) The spy likes to fry.

b) The spy likes to fly.

3.

a) The sky can pry.

b) The spy can pry.

4.

a) The fly can dry.

b) The fly can cry.

Zoo Review

Write the vowels to complete each word.

i_e   ie   y

1. d__m__

2. dr__

3. fr__

4. sh__

5. sk__

6. p__ __

7. t__ __

8. cr__

9. wh__

10. p__n__

11. d__v__

12. sp__

Find the Five

Find the five words that are shown in the picture and circle them. Cross out the words that are not shown in the picture.

bike	tie	fry	mice	pry
pipe	time	cry	hide	fly

Same or Different?

Say the name of each picture and write e or i. Circle the word "same" if both pictures in the pair make the same sound. Circle "different" if they make different sounds.

1. same different

2. same different

3. same different

4. same different

5. same different

6. same different

Race Time

Write the vowels to complete each word. Count the number of long e words and the number of long i words on the race track. Write the numbers in the boxes and see which letter wins!

 **Bone makes the long o sound.**

bone

Say the name of each picture and listen to the long o sound. Circle the letters o and e in each word.

cone

hose

note

pole

robe

rose

Now trace the letters o and e in each word.

rope

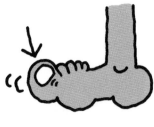
toe

hoe

Hidden Picture

Say the name of each picture. If it makes the long o sound, color the space.

Look at the pictures in the spaces you colored. Circle the words that name those pictures.

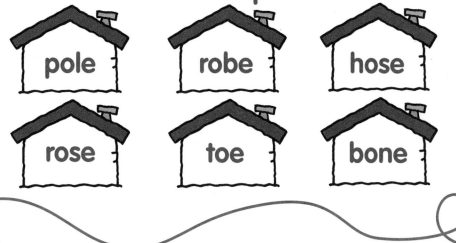

pole   robe   hose

rose   toe   bone

All Aboard

Say the name of each picture in the train. Find the word that matches each picture and write it on the line.

hoe
toe
hose

rope
rose
robe

bone
note
cone

Riddle and Rhyme

Read each riddle and look at the picture. Write the word to complete the riddle.

cone   hose   hoe

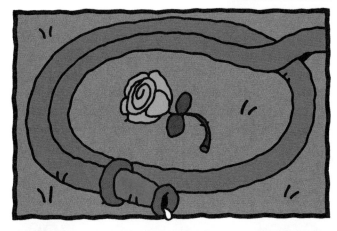

1. The rose is by the

   _____.

2. The bone is on the

   _____.

3. My toe is on the

   _____.

 **Boat makes the long o sound.**

boat

Say the name of each picture and listen to the long o sound. Circle the letters oa in each word.

float

goal

goat

loaf

oar

road

Now trace the letters oa in each word.

soap

toad

toast

Count Down

Circle the pictures whose names make the long o sound. Count the circled pictures on each rocket and write the number. Which rocket has the higher number?

Look at the circled pictures on the winning rocket. Circle the matching words.

oar

soap

toast

float

goal

All Aboard

Say the name of each picture in the train. Find the word that matches each picture and write it on the line.

loaf
goal
goat

toad
toast
soap

float
road
oar

Puzzle Time

Draw a line to match each picture with the correct sentence.

a) A goat is in the boat.

b) A loaf is in the road.

c) An oar is in the boat.

d) A toad is in the road.

OW

Bow makes the long o sound.

bow

Say the name of each picture and listen to the long o sound. Circle the letters ow in each word.

blow   crow   grow

low   mow   row

Now trace the letters ow in each word.

slow

snow

throw

Monkey Maze

Help the monkey find its way through the maze. Connect the pictures whose names make the long o sound.

Which pictures did you connect in the maze? Circle the words that name those pictures.

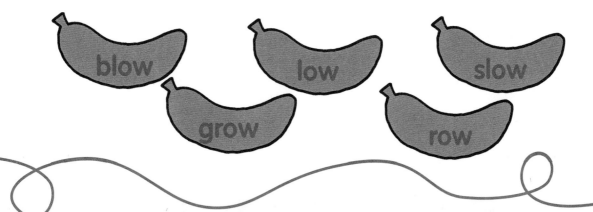

blow

low

slow

grow

row

All Aboard

Say the name of each picture in the train. Find the word that matches each picture and write it on the line.

low
blow
bow

slow
snow
mow

grow
throw
crow

Silly Sentences

Circle the sentence that matches each picture.

1.

a) The bow is on the crow.

b) The snow is on the crow.

2.

a) I try to row the snow.

b) I try to mow the snow.

3.

Now   Later

a) The crow will grow.

b) The bow will grow.

4.

a) I can row the snow.

b) I can throw the snow.

Zoo Review

Write the vowels to complete each word.

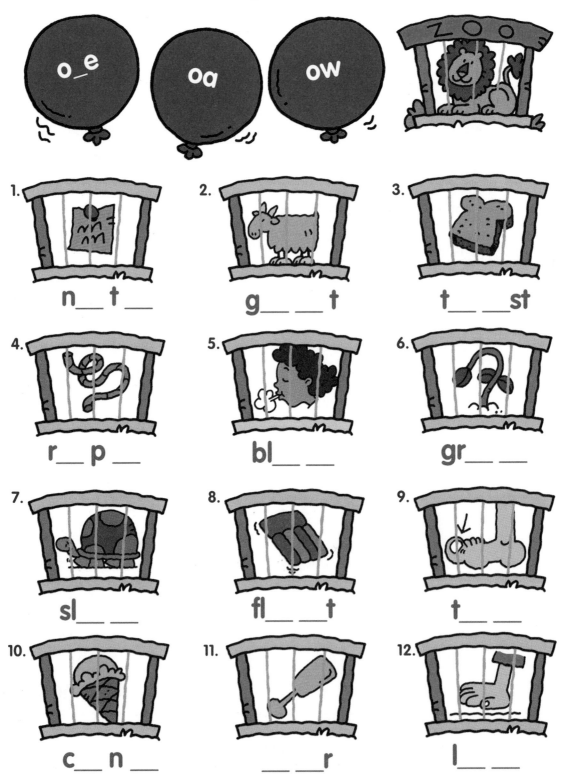

o_e

oa

ow

1. n__ t __

2. g__ __ t

3. t__ __st

4. r__ p __

5. bl__ __

6. gr__ __

7. sl__ __

8. fl__ __ t

9. t__ __

10. c__ n __

11. __ __ r

12. l__ __

Find the Five

Find the five words that are shown in the picture and circle them. Cross out the words that are not shown in the picture.

snow	bone	toad	toast	crow
hose	row	throw	bow	mow

Sounds and Signs

Say the name of each picture. Draw a line to connect the picture with i or o.

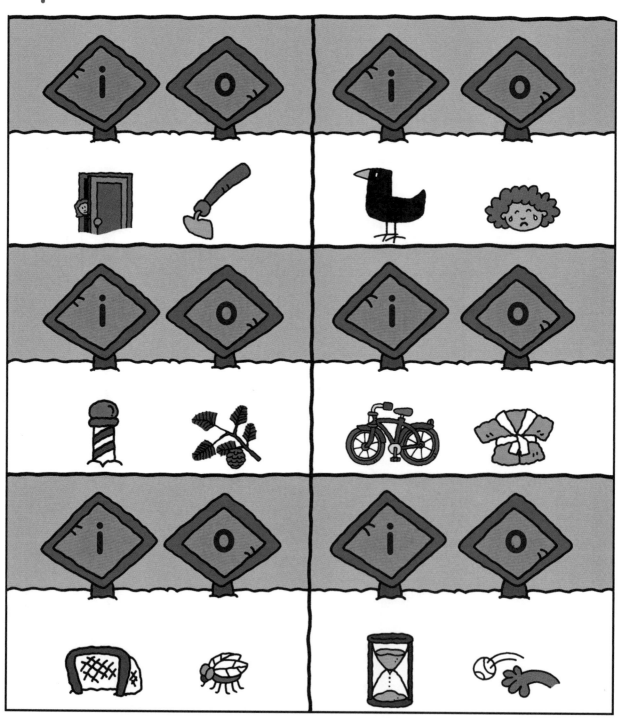

Hats Off!

Write the vowels to complete each word. Then match each hat with its owner. If the word has the long i sound, draw a line to Clive. If it has the long o sound, draw a line to Moe.

i_e   y   o_e
ow   oa

**u_e** **Tube makes the long u sound.**

tube

Say the name of each picture and listen to the long u sound. Circle the letters u and e in each word.

cube

mule

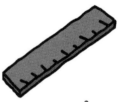
rule

June

tune

flute

Now trace the letters u and e in each word.

clue

blue

glue

Hidden Picture

Say the name of each picture. If it makes the long u sound, color the space.

Look at the pictures in the spaces you colored. Circle the words that name those pictures.

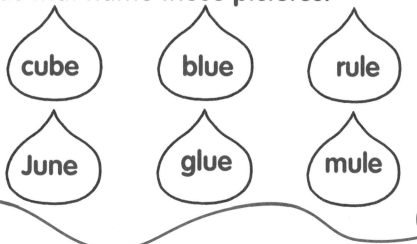

cube

blue

rule

June

glue

mule

All Aboard

Say the name of each picture in the train. Find the word that matches each picture and write it on the line.

clue
blue
glue

rule
mule
flute

tune
tube
June

Puzzle Time

Draw a line to match each picture with the correct sentence.

1.

a) The tube is on the cube.

2.

b) I play a tune on the flute.

3.

c) The mule is on the cube.

4.

d) I put glue on the flute.

Same or Different?

Say the name of each picture and write o or u. Circle the word "same" if both pictures in the pair make the same sound. Circle "different" if they make different sounds.

1. same different

2. same different

3. same different

4. same different

5. same different

6. same different

Race Time

Write the vowels to complete each word. Count the number of long o words and the number of long u words on the race track. Write the numbers in the boxes and see which letter wins!

Start

Finish

Scoreboard

o

U

1. cl___ ___

2. r___ s___

3. g___ t

thr___ ___

4.

5. gl___ ___

6. J___ n___

7. fl___ t___

8. m___ l___

Sounds and Signs

Say the name of each picture. Draw a line to connect the picture with long a or long u.

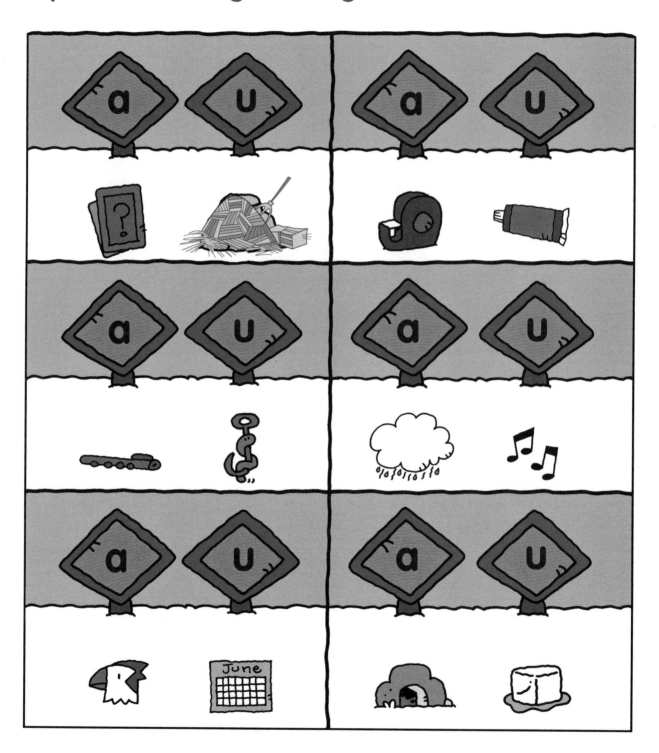

Hats Off!

Write the vowels to complete each word. Then match each hat with its owner. If the word has the long a sound, draw a line to Dave. If it has the long u sound, draw a line to Jules.

a_e   ai
ay   u_e

bl__ __ __

l__ k__

tr__ __ __n

s__ __ l

Dave

Jules

c__ n__ __

m__ l__ __

tr__ __ __

gl__ __ __

Rainy Review

Draw a line to connect the pictures whose names make the same vowel sound.

What Belongs in the Box?

Say the name of the pictures in each box. Cross out the picture whose name does not make the same sound as the other two. Then write the correct sound in the box.

a e i o u

Gumball Fun

Write the missing vowels for each word.

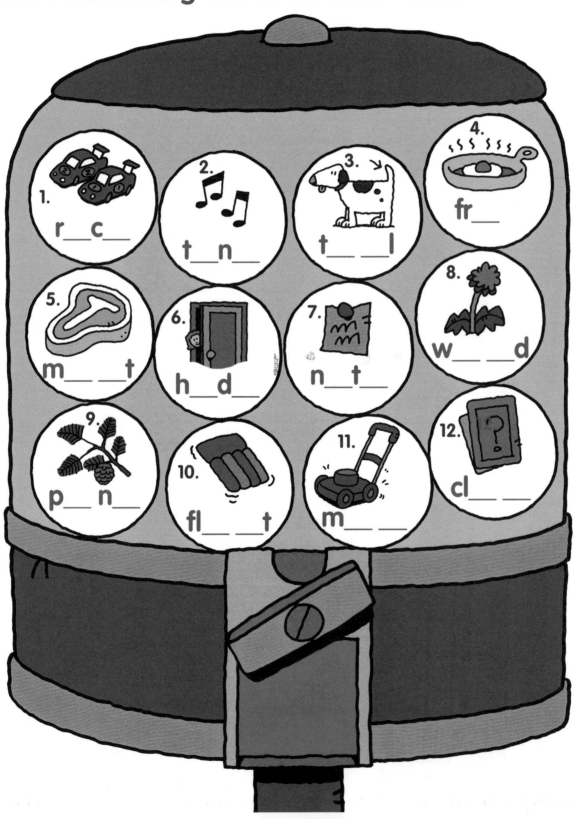

1. r__c__

2. t__n__

3. t____l

4. fr__

5. m____t

6. h__d__

7. n__t__

8. w____d

9. p__n__

10. fl____t

11. m____

12. cl____

Picture Search

Search the scene and find two pictures for each long vowel sound. Circle the pictures and write the words below.

skate	pail	tree	peach	pie
bike	rose	loaf	tube	flute

a   e   i   o   u

___ ___ ___ ___ ___

___ ___ ___ ___ ___

Which Word?

Circle the word that matches the picture. Then write the word on the line.

1. _____ cone cane

2. _____ three throw

3. _____ sleep slow

4. _____ wheel why

5. _____ pray pry

6. _____ tie tea

Crossword Puzzle

Use the picture clues to complete the puzzle.

Down

1.

2.

4.

5.

6.

8.

Across

1.

4.

3.

7.

9.

Story Time

Write the word to complete each sentence in the story.

> rain dive beach robe boat oar

1. I like to sail my _____.

2. _____ falls from the sky.

3. The _____ blows away.

4. I _____ into the sea.

5. I row to the _____.

6. I wear a _____ to get dry.

Picture This

Draw a line to match each sentence with the correct picture.

The fly is on the cake.
The fly is on the clay.

The crow is on the train.
The crow is in the tree.

The bee is on the rose.
The bow is on the rose.

Draw a picture to match each sentence. Connect the sentence and the picture.

The snail is on the hay.
Snow is on the hay.

Vowel Teams

Say the name of each picture. Count the number of players for each vowel sound and write the number below.

1.
2.
3.
4. $1+1=2$
5.
6.
7.
8.
9.
10.

short
a ____

long
a ____

Short and Long

Fill in the missing letters to complete each word.

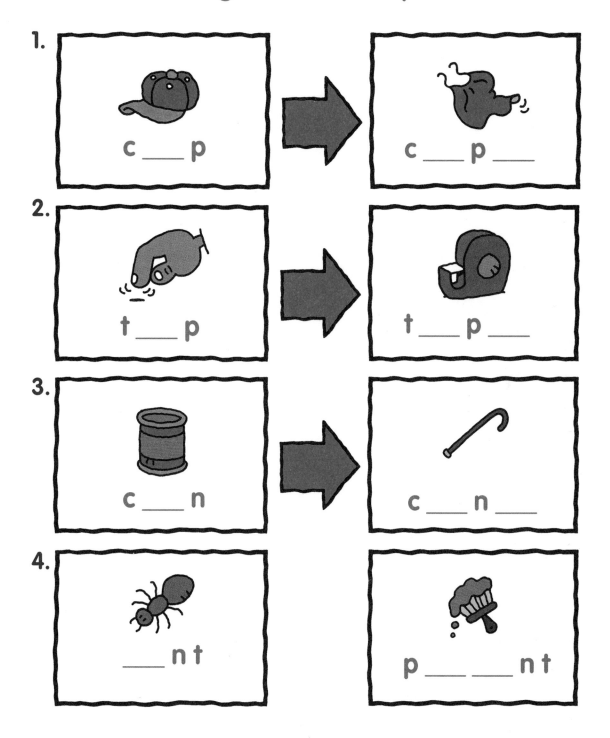

1. c___p → c___p___

2. t___p → t___p___

3. c___n → c___n___

4. ___n t → p___ ___n t

Picture Pages

For each page find two pictures whose names have the short a sound and three with the long a sound. Write the words on the right. Use the word box.

braid	jay	add	ant	wag
apple	tape	snail	rake	May

short a

_____ _____

long a

_____ _____

_____

short a

_____ _____

long a

_____ _____

_____

Riddle Review

Connect each riddle with the matching picture.

1. I am fast.
   I am in the race.

2. I wag my tail.

3. I am a cake.
   I am for Dad.

4. I tap on a tray.

Vowel Teams

Say the name of each picture. Count the number of players for each vowel sound and write the number below.

short e ____   long e ____

Measure Up

Fill in the missing vowels for each word.

1.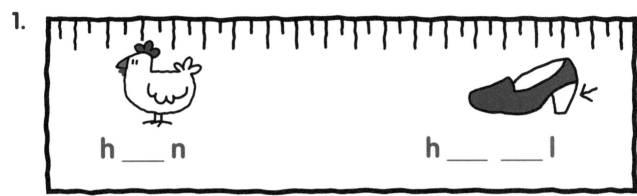

   h ___ n   h ___ ___ l

2.

   b ___ d   b ___ ___ d

3.

   w ___ t   w ___ ___ d

4.

   w ___ ll   wh ___ ___ l

Picture Pages

For each page find one picture whose name has the short e sound and two with the long e sound. Write the words on the right. Use the word box.

| tree | peach | tea |
| peel | egg | nest |

short e

_____

long e

_____ _____

short e

_____

long e

_____ _____

Photo Fun

Circle the word that makes sense and matches the photo.

1. We have three _____.

    legs   wheels

2. The _____ is wet.

    hen   sheep

3. We sleep in the _____.

    bed   bee

4. The seal has a _____.

    pea   pen

Vowel Teams

Say the name of each picture. Count the number of players for each vowel sound and write the number below.

Short and Long

Fill in the missing letters to complete each word.

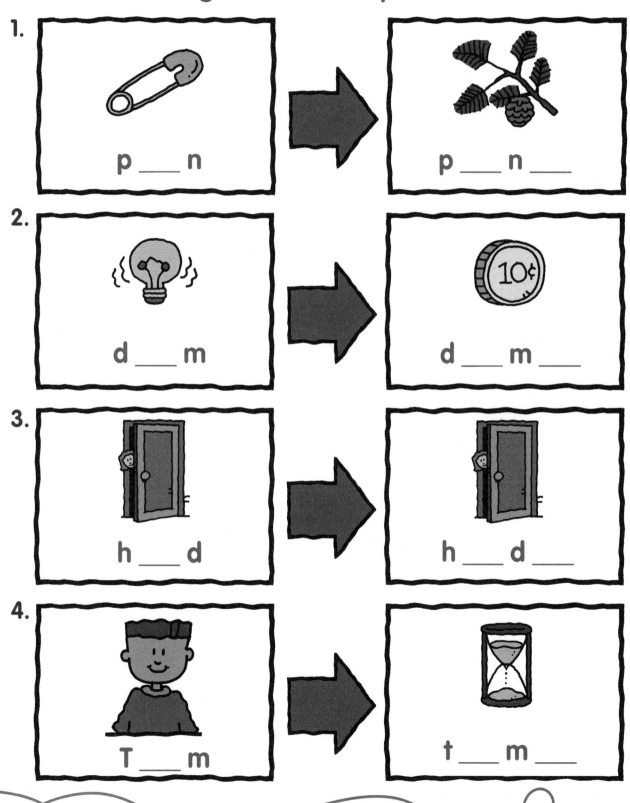

1. p___n   p___n___

2. d___m   d___m___

3. h___d   h___d___

4. T___m   t___m___

Picture Pages

For each page find one picture whose name has the short i sound and two with the long i sound. Write the words on the right. Use the word box.

sip	dry	fry	zip	mice	tie

short i

_____

long i

_____ _____

short i

_____

long i

_____ _____

Riddle Review

Connect each riddle with the matching picture.

1. I have a wig.
   I am a spy.

2. I sit on my bike.

3. I am a pig.
   I like pie.

4. I dive off the ship.

Vowel Teams

Say the name of each picture. Count the number of players for each vowel sound and write the number below.

Measure Up

Fill in the missing vowels for each word.

1.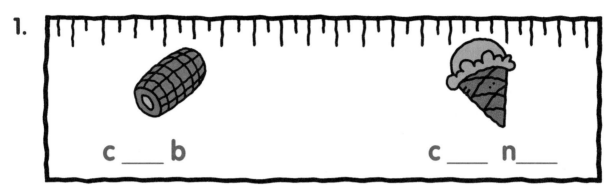

   c __ b   c __ n __

2.

   l __ g   l __ __

3.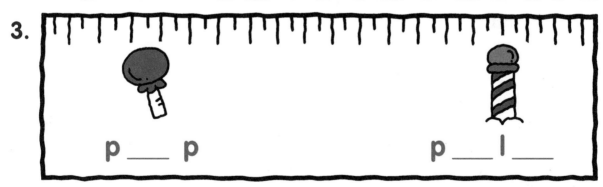

   p __ p   p __ l __

4.

   m __ m   m __ __

Picture Pages

For each page find two pictures whose name have the short o sound and three that have the long o sound. Write the words on the right. Use the word box.

bone	clock	toast	frog	mom
throw	jog	robe	goal	bow

short o

_____ _____

long o

_____ _____

_____

short o

_____ _____

long o

_____ _____

_____

Photo Fun

Circle the word that makes sense and matches the photo.

1. I float in the _____.

   pond   pole

2. Mom has a _____.

   loaf   log

3. The frog will _____.

   grow   jog

4. I pop the _____ bubble.

   stop   soap

Vowel Teams

Say the name of each picture. Count the number of players for each vowel sound and write the number below.

Short and Long

Fill in the missing letters to complete each word.

1. t___b → t___b___

2. c___b | c___b___

3. m___g | m___l___

4. j___mp | J___n___

Picture Pages

For each page find two pictures whose name have the short u sound and two that have the long u sound. Write the words on the right. Use the word box.

duck	mug	rule	flute
mule	plug	glue	sun

short u

_____ _____

long u

_____ _____

short u

_____ _____

long u

_____ _____

Riddle Review

Connect each riddle with the matching picture.

1. I have a plug.
   I play a tune.

2. I am a pup in glue.

3. I play a flute.
   I have fun.

4. I am a mule on a
   truck.

Picture Search

Search the scene and find as many pictures as you can for each vowel sound or pair. Write the words in the boxes.

short a

short e

short i

short o

short u

dad	pen	wet	can	ship	skate
pail	paint	spray	lock	bee	weed
peach	bead	bike	pipe	sky	fly
note	hose	boat	soap	bow	mow
glue	tube	mom	pup	sun	tape

long a

long e

long i

long o

long u

Crossword Puzzle

Use the picture clues to complete the puzzle.

Down

1.

3.

4.

7.

8.

9.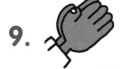

11.

13.

Across

2.

4.

5.

6.

8.

10.

11.

12.

Story Time

Read the story. Write the word to complete each sentence and match the picture.

say	hide	bed	snow	pup
toe	hay	clock	mice	cry

Mom will go _____.

It's time to _____,
"Here I come!"

I look in the _____.
It's my _____!

I look by the _____.
I see _____!

I want to sit and _____.

Then I see a clue in the _____.

I see a _____ and a bow.

Mom is asleep in the _____.

Answer Key

Page 5

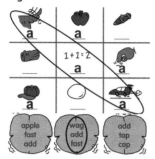

apple fast add	wag add fast	add tap cap

Page 6

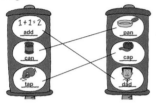

Page 7

4 The ant is on the apple.
3 Dad has a pan.
1 The ant is on the can.
2 Dad is fast.

Page 9

Page 10

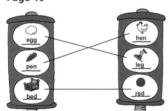

Page 11

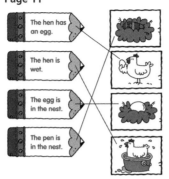

Page 12

1. e	a	different
2. e	a	different
3. a	a	same
4. e	e	same
5. e	e	same
6. e	a	different

Page 13

1. red
2. dad
3. can
4. hen
5. egg
6. apple
7. ant
8. cap

short a= 5
short e= 3

Page 15

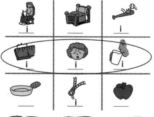

sick hit sip	sit sick zip	inch sick sip

Page 16

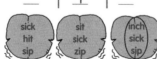

Page 17

4 The pig has a wig.
3 I swim to the ship.
2 The pig is on the ship.
1 I swim in a wig.

Page 18

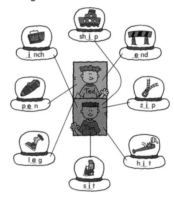

Page 19

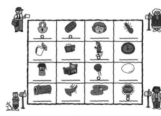

Page 21

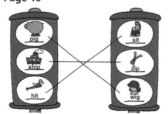

Page 22

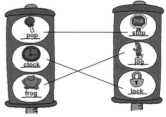

Page 23

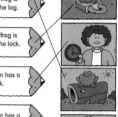

Page 24

1. o	i	different
2. o	i	different
3. o	o	same
4. o	i	different
5. o	o	same
6. i	i	same

Page 25

1. ship
2. sit
3. lock
4. zip
5. log
6. inch
7. pond
8. swim

short i = 5
short o = 3

Page 27

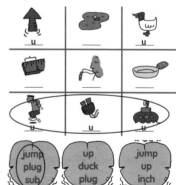

jump plug sub	up duck plug	jump up inch

Page 28

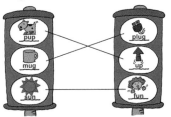

Page 29

<u>3</u> The duck is in the truck.
<u>4</u> The mug is in the sun.
<u>2</u> The pup is in the truck.
<u>1</u> The sub is in the sun.

Page 30

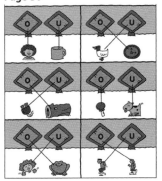

Page 31

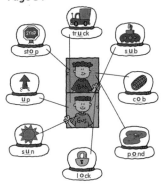

Page 32

1. a	u	different
2. u	u	same
3. a	a	same
4. u	a	different
5. a	a	same
6. u	a	different

Page 33

1. ant
2. jump
3. mug
4. apple
5. cap
6. plug
7. sub
8. sun

short u= 5
short a= 3

Page 34

Page 35

Page 36

1. plug
2. fun
3. hit
4. red
5. dad
6. zip
7. pen
8. wag
9. end
10. sub
11. frog

Page 37

Words in the picture include:

a	e	i	o	u
<u>can</u>	<u>wet</u>	<u>sip</u>	<u>cob</u>	<u>pup</u>
<u>apple</u>	<u>leg</u>	<u>zip</u>	<u>clock</u>	<u>sun</u>

Page 38

1. wig
2. pop
3. leg
4. nest
5. add
6. cap

Page 39

Down
1.
4.
5.
7.
8.

Across
2.
3.
6.
8.
9.

Page 40

1. The pup has my <u>cap</u>.
2. He is too <u>fast</u>.
3. He sees a <u>frog</u> jump.
4. Stop, pup. Don't <u>jump</u>!
5. The pup is in the <u>pond</u>.
6. Now my cap is all <u>wet</u>.

Page 41

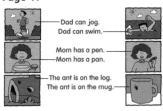

Dad can jog.
Dad can swim.

Mom has a pen.
Mom has a pan.

The ant is on the log.
The ant is on the mug.

Page 43

Page 44

Page 45

1. a
2. b
3. a
4. a

Page 47

Page 48

Page 48 illustration with train cars: bait, braid, paint, maid, tail, train, sail, snail, pail.

Page 49

1. The maid has a <u>braid</u>.
2. The snail is on the <u>pail</u>.
3. The train is in the <u>rain</u>.

Page 51

May pay spray say ray

Page 52

pay pray tray | pray | pay | tray
ray | say | spray | say spray ray
May hay jay | jay | May | hay

Page 53

1. b
2. c
3. a
4. d

Page 54

1. pay
2. race
3. paint
4. tail
5. pray
6. ray
7. bake
8. train
9. braid
10. tape
11. cane
12. say

Page 55

cave dake hay bait snail
pail sail jay cape cake

Page 57

Page 58

cheek sleep sheep | sleep | cheek | sheep
heel | weed | wheel | wheel heel weed
tree bee three | tree | bee | three

Page 59

1. b
2. a
3. b
4. a

Page 61

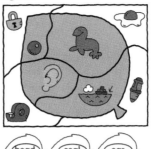

bead | seal | ear
sea | eat | beach

Page 62

beach bead peach | bead | peach | beach
pea | sea | seal | seal pea sea
meat eat ear | eat | meat | ear

Page 63

1. The peach is on the <u>beach</u>.
2. I like to eat the <u>meat</u>.
3. A pea is in the <u>tea</u>.

Page 64

1. three
2. cheek
3. eat
4. bead
5. heel
6. tree
7. sheep
8. meat
9. ear
10. tea
11. pea
12. peach

Page 65

sleep eat peel wheel bee
sea free weed beach bead

Page 66

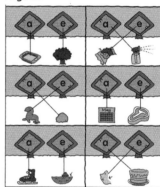

Page 67

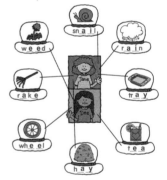

Page 69

tie dive hide dime time

Page 70

Page 71
1. d
2. c
3. a
4. b

Page 73

Page 74

Page 75
1. a
2. a
3. b
4. b

Page 76
1. dime
2. dry
3. fry
4. shy
5. sky
6. pie
7. tie
8. cry
9. why
10. pine
11. dive
12. spy

Page 77

Page 78
1. e   i   different
2. i   e   different
3. i   i   same
4. i   e   different
5. i   i   same
6. e   e   same

Page 79
1. dry
2. tie
3. fry
4. eat
5. ear
6. tree
7. hide
8. why

long e =3
long i=5

Page 81

Page 82

Page 83
1. The rose is by the <u>hose</u>.
2. The bone is on the <u>cone</u>.
3. My toe is on the <u>hoe</u>.

Page 85

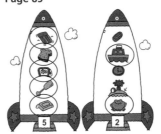

Page 86

Page 87
1. b
2. d
3. c
4. a

Page 89

Page 90

Page 91
1. a
2. b
3. a
4. b

Page 92
1. note
2. goat
3. toast
4. rope
5. blow
6. grow
7. slow
8. float
9. toe
10. cone
11. oar
12. low

Page 93

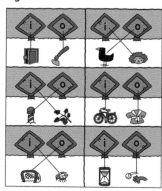

Page 94

Page 95

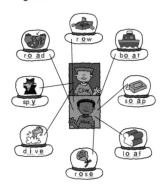

Page 97

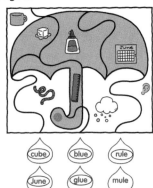

Page 98

Page 99
1. d
2. b
3. c
4. a

Page 100
1. u   o   different
2. o   o   same
3. u   o   different
4. o   o   same
5. u   u   same
6. o   u   different

Page 101
1. clue
2. rose
3. goat
4. throw
5. glue
6. June
7. flute
8. mule

long o= 3
long u= 5

Page 102

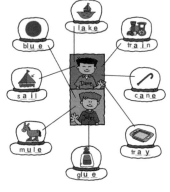

Page 103

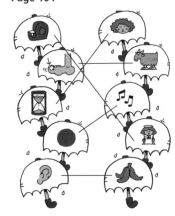

Page 104

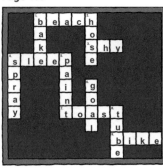

Page 105

Page 106
1. race
2. tune
3. tail
4. fry
5. meat
6. hide
7. note
8. weed
9. pine
10. float
11. mow
12. clue

Page 107

Words in the picture include:
a   e   i   o   u
skate   tree   pie   loaf   flute
pail   peach   bike   rose   tube

Page 108
1. cane
2. three
3. slow
4. wheel
5. pry
6. tea

Page 109

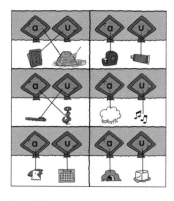

Page 110
1. I like to sail my boat.
2. Rain falls from the sky.
3. The oar blows away.
4. I dive into the sea.
5. I row to the beach.
6. I wear a robe to get dry.

Page 111

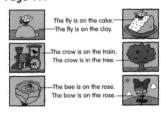

The fly is on the cake.
The fly is on the clay.

The crow is on the train.
The crow is in the tree.

The bee is on the rose.
The bow is on the rose.

Page 112
1. short a
2. long a
3. long a
4. short a
5. short a
6. long a
7. long a
8. long a
9. long a
10. short a

short a= 4
long a= 6

Page 113
1. cap; cape
2. tap; tape
3. can; cane
4. ant; paint

Page 114
Top:
short a:
wag
ant
long a:
rake
jay
snail

Bottom:
short a:
add
apple
long a:
braid
tape
May

Page 115
1. b
2. c
3. a
4. d

Page 116
1. long e
2. long e
3. short e
4. long e
5. short e
6. short e
7. short e
8. long e
9. long e
10. short e
short e=5
long e=5

Page 117
1. hen; heel
2. bed; bead
3. wet; weed
4. well; wheel

Page 118
Top:
short e:
nest
long e:
tree
peach

Bottom:
short e:
egg
long e:
tea
peel

Page 119
1. We have three legs.
2. The sheep is wet.
3. We sleep in the bed.
4. The seal has a pen.

Page 120
1. short i
2. short i
3. long i
4. long i
5. short i
6. short i
7. long i
8. long i
9. short i
10. short i

short i= 6
long i= 4

Page 121
1. pin; pine
2. dim; dime
3. hid; hide
4. Tim; time

Page 122
Top:
short i:
sip
long i:
fry
mice

Bottom:
short i:
zip
long i:
tie
dry

Page 123
1. c
2. b
3. d
4. a

Page 124
1. long o
2. short o
3. long o
4. long o
5. long o
6. long o
7. long o
8. long o
9. short o
10. short o

short o= 3
long o= 7

Page 125
1. cob; cone
2. log; low
3. pop; pole
4. mom; mow

Page 126
Top:
short o:
frog
jog
long o:
bone
goal
throw

Bottom:
short o:
clock
mom
long o:
robe
bow
toast

Page 127
1. I float in the pond.
2. Mom has a loaf.
3. The frog will grow.
4. I pop the soap bubble.

Page 128
1. long u
2. short u
3. long u
4. short u
5. short u
6. long u
7. long u
8. short u
9. short u
10. short u

short u = 6
long u = 4

Page 129
1. tub; tube
2. cob; cube
3. mug; mule
4. jump; June

Page 130
Top:
short:
duck
sun
long u:
flute
mule

Bottom:
short u:
plug
mug
short u:
glue
rule

Page 131
1. d
2. c
3. a
4. b

Pages 132-133
short a:
dad
can
short e:
wet
pen
short i:
ship
short o:
lock
mom
short u:
pup
sun
long a:
tape
skate
pail
paint
spray
long e:
bee
weed
peach
bead
long i:
bike
pipe
sky
fly
long o:
note
hose
boat
soap
bow
mow
long u:
glue
tube

Page 134-135

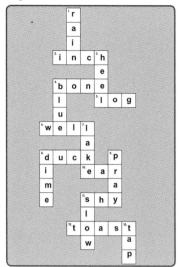

Pages 136-137
1. Mom will go <u>hide</u>.
2. It's time to <u>say</u>, "Here I come!"
3. I look in the <u>bed</u>. It's my <u>pup</u>!
4. I look by the <u>clock</u>. I see <u>mice</u>!
5. I want to sit and <u>cry</u>.
6. Then I see a clue in the <u>snow</u>.
7. I see a <u>toe</u> and a bow.
8. Mom is asleep in the <u>hay</u>.